Contents

1.
THE STUDY
OF ECONOMICS

The natural sciences are ultimately based on the facts as established by laboratory experiment. Physical and biological theories are confronted with these facts, and are rejected when in conflict with them. The perfection of these theories no less than the improvement of technological and therapeutical procedures requires more and better laboratory research. These experimental ventures absorb time, painstaking effort of specialists, and costly expenditure of material. Research can no longer be conducted by isolated and penniless scientists, however ingenious. The seat of experimentation today is in the huge laboratories supported by governments, universities, endowments, and big business. Work in these institutions has developed into professional routine. The majority of those employed in it are technicians recording those facts which the pioneers, of whom some are themselves experimenters, will one day use as building stones for their theories. As far as the progress of scientific theories is concerned, the achievements of the rank-and-file researcher are only ancillary. But very often his discoveries have immediate practical results in improving the methods of therapeutics and of business.

Ignoring the radical epistemological difference between the natural sciences and the sciences of human action, people believe that what is needed to further economic knowledge is to organize economic research according to the well-tried methods of the institutes for medical, physical, and chemical research. Considerable sums of money have been spent for what is labeled economic research. In fact the subject matter of the work of all these institutes is recent economic history.

It is certainly a laudable thing to encourage the study of economic history. However instructive the result of such studies may be, one must not confuse them with the study of economics. They do not produce facts in the sense in which this term is applied with regard to the events tested in laboratory experiments. They do not deliver bricks for the construction of *a posteriori* hypotheses and theorems. On the contrary, they are without meaning if not interpreted in the light of theories developed without reference to them. There is no need to add anything to what has been said in this respect in the preceding chapters. No controversy concerning the causes of a historical event can be solved on the ground of an examination of the facts which is not guided by definite praxeological theories.[1]

The foundation of institutes for cancer research can possibly contribute to the discovery of methods

---

[1]Cf., about the essential epistemological problems involved, pp. 31–40, about the problem of "quantitative" economics, pp. 55–57 and 347–49, and about the antagonistic interpretation of labor conditions under capitalism, pp. 613–18. [*These page references are to other sections in* Human Action.]

for fighting and preventing this per-
nicious disease. But a business cycle
research institute is of no help in
endeavors to avoid the recurrence of
depressions. The most exact and reliable assemblage of all the data concerning economic depressions of the
past is of little use for our knowledge
in this field. Scholars do not disagree
with regard to these data; they disagree with regard to the theorems to
be resorted to in their interpretation.

Still more important is the fact
that it is impossible to collect the data
concerning a concrete event without
reference to the theories held by the
historian at the very outset of his
work. The historian does not report
all facts, but only those which he
considers as relevant on the ground
of his theories; he omits data considered irrelevant for the interpretation
of the events. If he is misled by faulty

theories, his report becomes clumsy and may be almost worthless.

Even the most faithful examination of a chapter of economic history, though it be the history of the most recent period of the past, is no substitute for economic thinking. Economics, like logic and mathematics, is a display of abstract reasoning. Economics can never be experimental and empirical. The economist does not need an expensive apparatus for the conduct of his studies. What he needs is the power to think clearly and to discern in the wilderness of events what is essential from what is merely accidental.

There is no conflict between economic history and economics. Every branch of knowledge has its own merits and its own rights. Economists have never tried to belittle or deny the significance of economic history.

Neither do real historians object to the study of economics. The antagonism was intentionally called into being by the socialists and interventionists who could not refute the objections raised against their doctrines by the economists. The Historical School and the Institutionalists tried to displace economics and to substitute "empirical" studies for it precisely because they wanted to silence the economists. Economic history, as they planned it, was a means of destroying the prestige of economics and of propagandizing for interventionism.

2.
ECONOMICS
AS A PROFESSION

The early economists devoted themselves to the study of the problems of economics. In lecturing and writing books they were eager to communicate to their fellow citizens the results of their thinking. They tried to influence public opinion in order to make sound policies prevail in the conduct of civic affairs. They never conceived of economics as a profession.

The development of a profession of economists is an offshoot of interventionism. The professional economist is the specialist who is instrumental in designing various measures of government interference with business. He is an expert in the field of economic legislation, which today invariably aims at hindering the operation of the unhampered market economy.

There are thousands and thousands of such professional experts busy in the bureaus of the governments and of the various political parties and pressure groups and in the editorial offices of party newspapers and pressure group periodicals. Others are employed as advisers by business or run independent agencies. Some of them have nationwide or even worldwide reputations; many are among the most influential men of their country. It often happens that such experts are called to direct the affairs of big banks and corporations, are elected into the legislature, and are appointed as cabinet ministers. They rival the legal profession in the supreme conduct of political affairs. The eminent role they play is one of the most characteristic features of our age of interventionism.

There can be no doubt that a class of men who are so preponderant includes extremely talented individuals, even the most eminent men of our age. But the philosophy that guides their activities narrows their horizon. By virtue of their connection with definite parties and pressure groups, eager to acquire special privileges, they become one-sided. They shut their eyes to the remoter consequences of the policies they are advocating. With them nothing counts but the short-run concerns of the group they are serving. The ultimate aim of their efforts is to make their clients prosper at the expense of other people. They are intent upon convincing themselves that the fate of mankind coincides with the short-run interests of their group. They try to sell this idea to the public. In fighting for a higher price of silver, of wheat, or of sugar, for higher wages for the members of their union, or for a tariff on cheaper foreign products, they claim to be fighting for the supreme good, for liberty and justice, for their nation's flowering, and for civilization.

The public looks askance upon the lobbyists and blames them for the dismal features of interventionist legislation. However, the seat of the evil is much deeper. The philosophy of the various pressure groups has penetrated the legislative bodies. There are in the present-day parliaments representatives of wheat growers, of cattle breeders, of farmers' cooperatives, of silver, of the various labor unions, of industries which cannot stand foreign competition without tariffs, and of many other pressure groups. There are few for whom the nation counts more than their pressure group. The same holds true for the departments of the administration. The cabinet minister of agriculture considers himself the champion of the interests of farming; his main objective is to make food prices soar. The minister of labor considers himself the advocate of labor unions; his foremost aim is to make the unions as formidable as possible. Each department follows its own course and works against the endeavors of the other departments.

Many people complain today about the lack of creative statesmanship. However, under the predominance of interventionist ideas, a political career is open only to men who identify themselves with the interests of a pressure group. The mentality of a union leader or of a secretary of farmers' associations is not what is required for a far-sighted statesman. Service to the short-run interests of a pressure group is not conducive to the development of those qualities which make a great statesman. Statesmanship is invariably long-run policy; but pressure groups do not bother about the long run. The lamentable failure of the German Weimar system and of the Third Republic in France was primarily due to the fact that their politicians were merely experts in pressure group interests.

3.
FORECASTING AS A PROFESSION

When the businessmen finally learned that the boom created by credit expansion cannot last and must necessarily lead to a slump, they realized that it was important for them to know in time the date of the break. They turned to the economists for advice.

The economist knows that the boom must result in a depression. But he does not and cannot know when the crisis will appear. This depends on the special conditions of each case. Many political events can influence the outcome. There are no rules according to which the duration of the boom or of the following depression can be computed. And even if such rules were available, they would be of no use to business-men. What the individual business-man needs in order to avoid losses is knowledge about the date of the turning point at a time when other businessmen still believe that the crash is farther away than is really the case. Then his superior knowl-edge will give him the opportunity to arrange his own operations in such a way as to come out unharmed. But if the end of the boom could be calculated according to a formula, all businessmen would learn the date at the same time. Their endeavors to adjust their conduct of affairs to this information would immediately result in the appearance of all the phenomena of the depres-sion. It would be too late for any of them to avoid being victimized.

If it were possible to calculate the future structure of the market, the future would not be uncertain. There would be neither entrepreneurial loss nor profit. What people expect from the economists is beyond the power of any mortal man.

The very idea that the future is predictable, that some formulas could be substituted for the specific understanding which is the essence of entrepreneurial activity, and that familiarity with these formulas could make it possible for anybody to take over the conduct of business is, of course, an outgrowth of the whole complex of fallacies and misconceptions which are at the bottom of present-day anticapitalistic policies. There is in the whole body of what is called the Marxian philosophy not the slightest reference to the fact that the main task of action is to provide for the events of an *uncertain* future. The fact that the terms promoter and speculator are today used only with an opprobrious connotation clearly shows that our contemporaries do not even suspect in what the fundamental problem of action consists.

Entrepreneurial judgment is one of those things that cannot be bought on the market. The entrepreneurial idea that carries on and brings profit is precisely that idea which did not occur to the majority. It is not correct foresight as such that yields profits, but foresight better than that of the rest. The prize goes only to those dissenters who do not let themselves be misled by the errors accepted by the multitude. What makes profits emerge is the provision for future needs for which others have neglected to make adequate provision.

Entrepreneurs and capitalists expose their own material well-being if they are fully convinced of the soundness of their plans. They would never venture to take their economic life into their hands because an expert advised them to do so. Those ignorant people who operate on the stock and commodity exchanges according to tips are destined to lose their money, from whatever source they may have got their inspiration and "inside" information.

In fact both the economists and the businessmen are fully aware of the uncertainty of the future. The businessmen realize that the economists do not dispense any reliable information about things to come and that all that they provide is interpretation of statistical data referring to the past. For the capitalists and entrepreneurs the economists' opinions about the future count only as questionable conjectures. They are skeptical and not easily fooled. But as they quite correctly believe that it is useful to know all the data which could possibly have any relevance for their affairs, they subscribe to the newspapers and periodicals publishing the forecasts. Anxious not to neglect any source of information available, big business employs staffs of economists and statisticians.

Business forecasting fails in the vain attempts to make the uncertainty of the future disappear and to deprive entrepreneurship of its inherent speculative character. But it renders very valuable services in assembling and interpreting the available data about economic trends and developments of the recent past.

4.

ECONOMICS
AND THE UNIVERSITIES

Tax-supported universities are under the sway of the party in power. The authorities try to appoint only professors who are ready to advance ideas of which they themselves approve. As all nonsocialist governments are today firmly committed to interventionism, they appoint only interventionists. In their opinion, the first duty of the university is to sell the official social philosophy to the rising generation.[2] They have no use for economists.

---

[2]G. Santayana, in speaking of a professor of philosophy of the—then Royal Prussian—University of Berlin, observed that it seemed to this man "that a professor's business was to trudge along

24

However, interventionism prevails also at many of the independent universities.

According to an age-old tradition the objective of the universities is not only teaching, but also the promotion of knowledge and science. The duty of the university teacher is not merely to hand down to the students the complex of knowledge developed by other men. He is supposed to contribute to the enlargement of this treasure by his own work. It is assumed that he is a full-fledged member of the world-embracing republic of scholarship, an innovator and a pioneer on the road toward more and better knowledge. No university would admit that the

the governmental towpath with a legal cargo." (*Persons and Places* [New York, 1945], II, 7.)

members of its faculty are inferior to anybody in their respective fields. Every university professor considers himself equal to all other masters of his science. Like the greatest of them, he too contributes his share to the advancement of learning.

This idea of the equality of all professors is, of course, fictitious. There is an enormous difference between the creative work of the genius and the monograph of a specialist. Yet in the field of empirical research it is possible to cling to this fiction. The great innovator and the simple routinist resort in their investigations to the same technical methods of research. They arrange laboratory experiments or collect historical documents. The outward appearance of their work is the same. Their publications refer to the same subjects and problems. They are commensurable.

It is quite otherwise in theoretical sciences like philosophy and economics. Here there is nothing that the routinist can achieve according to a more or less stereotyped pattern. There are no tasks which require the conscientious and painstaking effort of sedulous monographers. There is no empirical research; all must be achieved by the power to reflect, to meditate, and to reason. There is no specialization, as all problems are linked with one another. In dealing with any part of the body of knowledge one deals actually with the whole. An eminent historian once described the psychological and educational significance of the doctoral thesis by declaring that it gives the author the proud assurance that there is a little corner, although small, in the field of learning in the knowledge of which he is second to none. It is obvious that this effect cannot be realized by a thesis on a subject of economic analysis. There are no such isolated corners in the complex of economic thought.

There never lived at the same time more than a score of men whose work contributed anything essential to economics. The number of creative men is as small in economics as it is in other fields of learning. Besides, many of the creative economists do not belong to the teaching profession. But there is a demand for thousands of university and college teachers of economics. Scholastic tradition requires that each of them should attest his worth by the publication of original contributions, not merely by compiling textbooks and manuals. An academic teacher's reputation and salary depend more on his literary work than on his didactic abilities. A professor cannot help publishing books. If he does not feel the vocation to write on economics, he turns to economic history or descriptive economics. But then, in order not to lose face, he must insist on the claim that the problems he treats are economics proper, not economic history. He must even pretend that his writings cover the only legitimate field of economic studies, that they alone are empirical, inductive, and scientific, while the merely deductive outpourings of the "armchair" theorists are idle speculations. If he were to neglect this, he would admit that there are among the teachers of economics two classes—those who themselves have contributed to the advancement of economic thought and those who have not, although they may have done a fine job in other disciplines such as recent economic history. Thus the academic atmosphere becomes unpropitious for the teaching of economics. Many professors–happily not all of them—are intent upon disparaging "mere theory." They try to substitute an unsystematically assembled collection of historical and statistical information for economic analysis. They dissolve economics into a number of integrated branches. They specialize in agriculture, in labor, in Latin American conditions, and in many other similar subdivisions.

It is certainly one of the tasks of university training to make students familiar with economic history in general and no less with recent economic developments. But all such endeavors are doomed to failure if not firmly grounded upon a thorough acquaintance with economics.

Economics does not allow of any breaking up into special branches. It invariably deals with the interconnectedness of all the phenomena of action. The catallactic problems cannot become visible if one deals with each branch of production separately. It is impossible to study labor and wages without studying implicitly commodity prices, interest rates, profit and loss, money and credit, and all the other major problems. The real problems of the determination of wage rates cannot even be touched in a course on labor. There are no such things as "economics of labor" or "economics of agriculture." There is only one coherent body of economics.

What these specialists deal with in their lectures and publications is not economics, but the doctrines of the various pressure groups. Ignoring economics, they cannot help falling prey to the ideologies of those aiming at special privileges for their group. Even those specialists who do not openly side with a definite pressure group and who claim to maintain a lofty neutrality unwittingly endorse the essential creeds of the interventionist doctrine. Dealing exclusively with the innumerable varieties of government interference with business, they do not want to cling to what they call mere negativism. If they criticize the measures resorted to, they do it only in order to recommend their own brand of interventionism as a substitute for other people's interventionism. Without a qualm they endorse the fundamental theses of both interventionism and socialism that the unhampered market economy unfairly harms the vital interests of the immense majority for the sole benefit of callous exploiters. As they see it, an economist who demonstrates the futility of interventionism is a bribed champion of the unjust claims of big business. It is imperative to bar such scoundrels from access to the universities and their articles from being printed in the periodicals of the associations of university teachers.

The students are bewildered. In the courses of the mathematical economists they are fed formulas describing hypothetical states of equilibrium in which there is no longer any action. They easily conclude that these equations are of no use whatever for the comprehension of economic activities. In the lectures of the specialists they hear a mass of detail concerning interventionist measures. They must infer that conditions are paradoxical indeed, because there is never equilibrium, and wage rates and the prices of farm products are not so high as the unions or the farmers want them to be. It is obvious that a radical reform is indispensable. But what kind of reform?

The majority of the students espouse without any inhibitions the interventionist panaceas recommended by their professors. Social conditions will be perfectly satisfactory when the government enforces minimum wage rates and provides everybody with adequate food and housing, or when the sale of margarine and the importation of foreign sugar are prohibited. They do not see the contradictions in the words of their teachers, who one day lament the madness of competition and the next day the evils of monopoly, who one day complain about falling prices and the next day about rising living costs. They take their degrees and try as soon as possible to get a job with the government or a powerful pressure group.

But there are many young men who are keen enough to see through the fallacies of interventionism. They accept their teachers' rejection of the unhampered market economy. But they do not believe that the isolated measures of interventionism could succeed in attaining the ends sought. They consistently carry their preceptors' thoughts to their ultimate logical consequences. They turn toward socialism. They hail the Soviet system as the dawn of a new and better civilization.

However, what has made many of the present-day universities by and large nurseries of socialism is not so much the conditions prevailing in the departments of economics as the teachings handed down in other departments. In the departments of economics there can still be found eminent economists, and even the other teachers are familiar with some of the objections raised against the practicability of socialism. The case is different with many of the teachers of philosophy, history, literature, sociology, and political science. They interpret history on the ground of a garbled vulgarization of dialectical materialism. Even many of those who passionately attack Marxism on account of its materialism and atheism are under the sway of the ideas developed in the *Communist Manifesto* and in the program of the Communist International. They explain depressions, mass unemployment, inflation, war and poverty as evils necessarily inherent in capitalism and intimate that these phenomena can disappear only with the passing of capitalism.

5.
GENERAL EDUCATION AND ECONOMICS

In countries which are not harassed by struggles between various linguistic groups public education can work very well if it is limited to reading, writing, and arithmetic. With bright children it is even possible to add elementary notions of geometry, the natural sciences, and the valid laws of the country. But as soon as one wants to go farther, serious difficulties appear. Teaching at the elementary level necessarily turns into indoctrination. It is not feasible to represent to adolescents all the aspects of a problem and to let them choose between dissenting views. It is no less impossible to find teachers who could hand down opinions of which they themselves disapprove in such a way as to satisfy those who hold these opinions. The party that operates the schools is in a position to propagandize its tenets and to disparage those of other parties.

In the field of religious education the liberals solved this problem by the separation of state and church. In liberal countries religion is no longer taught in public schools. But the parents are free to send their children into denominational schools supported by religious communities.

However, the problem does not refer only to the teaching of religion and of certain theories of the natural sciences at variance with the Bible. It concerns even more the teaching of history and economics.

The public is aware of the matter only with regard to the international aspects of the teaching of history. There is some talk today about the necessity of freeing the teaching of history from the impact of nationalism and chauvinism. But few people realize that the problem of impartiality and objectivity is no less present in dealing with the domestic aspects of history. The teacher's or the textbook author's own social philosophy colors the narrative. The more the treatment must be simplified and condensed in order to be comprehensible to the immature minds of children and adolescents, the worse are the effects.

As the Marxians and the interventionists see it, the teaching of history in the schools is tainted by the endorsement of the ideas of old liberalism. They want to substitute their own interpretation of history for the "bourgeois" interpretation. In Marxian opinion the English Revolution of 1688, the American Revolution, the great French Revolution, and the nineteenth-century revolutionary movements in continental Europe were bourgeois movements. They resulted in the defeat of feudalism and in the establishment of bourgeois supremacy. The proletarian masses were not emancipated; they merely passed from the class rule of the aristocracy to the class rule of the capitalist exploiters. To free the working man, the abolition of the capitalist mode of production is required. This, contend the interventionists, should be brought about by *Sozialpolitik* or the New Deal. The orthodox Marxians, on the other hand, assert that only the violent overthrow of the bourgeois system of government could effectively emancipate the proletarians.

It is impossible to deal with any chapter of history without taking a definite stand on these controversial issues and the implied economic doctrines. The textbooks and the teachers cannot adopt a lofty neutrality with regard to the postulate that the "unfinished revolution" needs to be completed by the communist revolution. Every statement concerning events of the last three hundred years involves a definite judgment on these controversies. One cannot avoid choosing between the philosophy of the Declaration of Independence and the Gettysburg Address and that of the *Communist Manifesto*. The challenge is there, and it is useless to bury one's head in the sand.

On the high school level and even on the college level the handing down of historical and economic knowledge is virtually indoctrination. The greater part of the students are certainly not mature enough to form their own opinions on the ground of a critical examination of their teachers' representation of the subject.

If public education were more efficient than it really is, the political parties would urgently aim at the domination of the school system in order to determine the mode in which these subjects are to be taught. However, general education plays only a minor role in the formation of the political, social, and economic ideas of the rising generation. The impact of the press, the radio, and environmental conditions is much more powerful than that of teachers and textbooks. The propaganda of the churches, the political parties, and the pressure groups outstrips the

influence of the schools, whatever
they may teach. What is learned in
school is often very soon forgotten
and cannot carry on against the con-
tinuous hammering of the social
milieu in which a man moves.

6.

ECONOMICS
AND THE CITIZEN

Economics must not be relegated
to classrooms and statistical offices
and must not be left to esoteric cir-
cles. It is the philosophy of human
life and action and concerns everybody and everything. It is the pith of
civilization and of man's human
existence.

To mention this fact is not to
indulge in the often derided weakness

of specialists who overrate the importance of their own branch of knowledge. Not the economists, but all the people today assign this eminent place to economics.

All present-day political issues concern problems commonly called economic. All arguments advanced in contemporary discussion of social and public affairs deal with fundamental matters of praxeology and economics. Everybody's mind is preoccupied with economic doctrines. Philosophers and theologians seem to be more interested in economic problems than in those problems which earlier generations considered the subject matter of philosophy and theology. Novels and plays today treat all things human—including sex relations—from the angle of economic doctrines. Everybody thinks of economics whether he is aware of it or not. In joining a political party and in casting his ballot, the citizen implicitly takes a stand upon essential economic theories.

In the sixteenth and seventeenth centuries religion was the main issue in European political controversies. In the eighteenth and nineteenth centuries in Europe as well as in America the paramount question was representative government versus royal absolutism. Today it is the market economy versus socialism. This is, of course, a problem the solution of which depends entirely on economic analysis. Recourse to empty slogans or to the mysticism of dialectical materialism is of no avail.

There is no means by which anyone can evade his personal responsibility. Whoever neglects to examine to the best of his abilities all the problems involved voluntarily surrenders his birthright to a self-appointed elite of supermen. In such vital matters blind reliance upon "experts" and uncritical acceptance of popular catchwords and prejudices is tantamount to the abandonment of self-determination and to yielding to other people's domination. As conditions are today, nothing can be more important to every intelligent man than economics. His own fate and that of his progeny is at stake.

Very few are capable of contributing any consequential idea to the body of economic thought. But all reasonable men are called upon to familiarize themselves with the teachings of economics. This is, in our age, the primary civic duty.

Whether we like it or not, it is a fact that economics cannot remain an esoteric branch of knowledge accessible only to small groups of scholars and specialists. Economics deals with society's fundamental problems; it concerns everyone and belongs to all. It is the main and proper study of every citizen.

7.
ECONOMICS AND FREEDOM

The paramount role that economic ideas play in the determination of civic affairs explains why governments, political parties, and pressure groups are intent upon restricting the freedom of economic thought. They are anxious to propagandize the "good" doctrine and to silence the voice of the "bad" doctrines. As they see it, truth has no inherent power which could make it ultimately prevail solely by virtue of its being true. In order to carry on, truth needs to be backed by violent action on the part of the police or other armed troops. In this view, the criterion of a doctrine's truth is the fact that its supporters succeeded in defeating by force of arms the champions of dissenting views. It is implied that God or some mythical agency directing the course of human affairs always bestows victory upon those fighting for the good cause. Government is from God and has the sacred duty of exterminating the heretic.

It is useless to dwell upon the contradictions and inconsistencies of this doctrine of intolerance and persecution of dissenters. Never before has the world known such a cleverly contrived system of propaganda and oppression as that instituted by contemporary governments, parties, and pressure groups. However, all these edifices will crumble like houses of cards as soon as a great ideology attacks them.

Not only in the countries ruled by barbarian and neobarbarian despots, but no less in the so-called Western democracies, the study of economics is practically outlawed today. The public discussion of economic problems ignores almost entirely all that has been said by economists in the last two hundred years. Prices, wage rates, interest rates, and profits are dealt with as if their determination were not subject to any law. Governments try to decree and to enforce maximum commodity prices and minimum wage rates. Statesmen exhort businessmen to cut down profits, to lower prices, and to raise wage rates as if these were dependent on the laudable intentions of individuals. In the treatment of international economic relations people blithely resort to the most naive fallacies of Mercantilism. Few are aware of the shortcomings of all these popular doctrines, or realize why the policies based upon them invariably spread disaster.

These are sad facts. However, there is only one way in which a man can respond to them: by never relaxing in the search for truth.

INDEX

Compiled by Richard Perry

About the Author

In six decades of teaching and 25 books, Ludwig von Mises (1881–1973) showed that government intervention is always destructive, whether through welfare, inflation, taxation, regulation, or war. His vision of the free, peaceful, and prosperous commonwealth is carried forward by the Mises Institute through teaching, publications, and scholarship.

Please note: All 900 pages of Mises's greatest work, *Human Action*—from which this chapter is taken—are available online at Mises.org. You can also order the spectacular Scholar's Edition of the book at the same website.